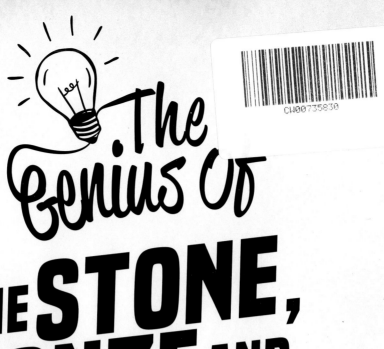

The Genius Of

THE STONE, BRONZE AND IRON AGES

CLEVER IDEAS AND INVENTIONS FROM PAST CIVILISATIONS

IZZI HOWELL

W

Franklin Watts

First published in Great Britain in 2019 by
The Watts Publishing Group

Copyright © The Watts Publishing Group, 2019

Produced for Watts by
White-Thomson Publishing Ltd
www.wtpub.co.uk

Series Editor: Izzi Howell
Consultant: Philip Parker
Series Designer: Rocket Design (East Anglia) Ltd
Designer: Clare Nicholas

ISBN: 978 1 4451 6046 7 (HB)   978 1 4451 6047 4 (PB)
10 9 8 7 6 5 4 3 2 1

Franklin Watts
An imprint of
Hachette Children's Group
Part of The Watts Publishing Group
Carmelite House
50 Victoria Embankment
London EC4Y 0DZ

An Hachette UK Company
www.hachette.co.uk

www.franklinwatts.co.uk

Printed in China

Picture acknowledgements:
Alamy: Heritage Image Partnership Ltd 7b, North Wind Picture Archives 9r, INTERFOTO 16, Ladi Kirn 23b; Getty: JUSTIN TALLIS/AFP 4t, HomoCosmicos 5b, Maltaguy1 10, English Heritage/Heritage Images 11t, 11b, 13 and 17, A-S-L 12br, Dean Mouhtaropoulos 19, De Agostini Picture Library/De Agostini 22, Henglein and Steets 28; Julian Baker 23t; Metropolitan Museum (public domain): Rogers Fund, 1999 3b and 25b, Dodge Fund, 1933 21t and 25t; Shutterstock: Brian C. Weed cover, Jule_Berlin title page and 18, pzAxe 3t, dikobraziy 4b, Diego Fiore 3t, Jason Benz Bennee 3c, arka38 6, mountainpix 7t, hapelena 8, Alena Brozova 9l, Alex Coan 12t, Alfonso de Tomas 12bl, Philip Bird LRPS CPAGB 14, Mr Nai 15 and 30, UAV 4 17, Bjoern Wylezich 20l, ntv 20r, Nataliya Nazarova 21b, EQRoy 24, Kamira 26, Fedor Selivanov 29; Walters Art Museum: Museum purchase, 1941 28c.

All design elements from Shutterstock.

CONTENTS

THE STONE, BRONZE AND IRON AGES

Who?

The Stone, Bronze and Iron Ages cover a long period of history. They stretch from the time of the first ancestors of modern humans, who lived millions of years ago, through to the first humans (*Homo sapiens*) and up until the time of the ancient civilisations. It was a period of great discovery and change, as humans began to use tools, grow crops and work with metal. These inventions had a huge impact on prehistoric society.

This is a reconstruction of the face of a man who lived in Britain 10,000 years ago. The man's skin, eye and hair colour is based on his DNA.

This map shows how and when humans travelled out of Africa and spread across the globe.

4–6 thousand years ago

40–45 thousand years ago

15–18 thousand years ago

60–65 thousand years ago

15 thousand years ago

50–55 thousand years ago

What happened?

The names 'Stone Age', 'Bronze Age' and 'Iron Age' are terms that historians use to divide up different stages in history that have certain characteristics. The Stone Age is characterised by the use of stone tools, while people worked with bronze during the Bronze Age, and began to use iron tools in the Iron Age.

This Bronze Age pottery model of a horse-drawn chariot was found in the remains of a Bronze Age town in what is now Lebanon.

Bronze and Iron Age people also worked with other metals, such as gold. This Iron Age gold neck-ring was found buried in Britain.

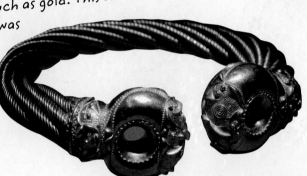

Where?

The Stone, Bronze and Iron Ages began and finished at different times across the world. For example, the Iron Age began 500 years earlier in the Middle East than in Europe. In Europe, the end of the Iron Age is considered the start of great ancient civilisations, such as the ancient Greeks and Romans. Some areas never went through certain periods. People in South America did not work with bronze or iron, and therefore didn't experience the Bronze or Iron Ages.

The Great Ziggurat of Ur was built by the Sumerians in Mesopotamia (modern-day Iraq) in the Bronze Age. The building has been restored to show what it would have looked like thousands of years ago.

STONE

The ancestors of modern humans began to use stones as tools around 3.3 million years ago in Africa. This moment marked the beginning of the Stone Age. During the Stone Age, humans learned how to turn stones into useful and ever more accurate tools.

GENIUS FIRST TOOLS

Chipping away

The very first stone tools were stones that had been naturally chipped. Humans used the sharp chipped edge as a cutting tool. It took time to find rocks that were naturally chipped, so people began to chip the rocks themselves to create cutting tools. They used another stone to chip away flakes of rock from one side of a round stone. This created a rough serrated edge that could be used to cut meat or dig roots out of the ground.

Early stone tools had rough, irregular blades.

(((BRAIN WAVE)))

The first stone tool-makers used a hard stone to shape tools. Later, they worked out that some rocks could be chipped using softer materials. One technique was to use a long piece of bone or horn to gently chip away very small pieces of rock. This created a much smoother blade.

Axes and beyond

Over time, humans worked out that chipping away both sides of a stone made a sharper, more effective blade. These tools were known as hand axes. Humans took the idea of the hand axe and developed it into different types of blade, such as knives, arrowheads and tools for scraping. These blades could cut through wood, bone and horn.

Sophisticated stones

Adding handles to stone tools made them much easier to hold. It also meant that they could be swung, which enabled people to apply more pressure when cutting. This helped them to cut up thick tree trunks. Stone Age people also learned how to make smoother tools by polishing them on a rough rock. A smooth blade was sharper, which meant that it could cut deeper and more accurately.

This Stone Age hand axe has two sharpened sides. It is made from flint, a type of rock that was often used for tools in the Stone Age.

To keep up with the demand for flint tools, Stone Age people mined flint from the ground. This drawing shows Grime's Graves, a flint mine in Britain. There, miners dug deep holes and picked flint out of the ground using horn tools.

BRONZE

In around 4000 BCE, in what is now Turkey and Bulgaria, the prehistoric world took a huge step forward when people started to produce bronze. By 2000 BCE, bronze-working technology and tools had spread across Europe and the Middle East.

pure copper

Copper

Before people started using bronze, they worked with copper. Getting hold of pure copper was fairly simple, as solid pieces of pure copper can sometimes be found in nature. However, copper was too soft for weapons and tools. So, people experimented with copper and learned that they could produce a much stronger metal by combining it with other substances. The resulting metal was bronze.

(((BRAIN WAVE)))

Bronze is an alloy – a mixture of different elements, including at least one metal. Bronze is mainly made up of copper, to which other elements are added. The first bronze was made by combining copper with arsenic (a poisonous substance). Later, people worked out that combining copper with tin made a stronger bronze alloy.

Melting and moulds

To make bronze, metal workers had to extract pure metal from copper and tin ores (rocks that contain metals and other substances). First, they crushed the ore into small pieces. Then, they heated the ore over a charcoal fire to melt the metal. The melted metal could then be separated from the rock and mixed with other substances to make bronze. The molten bronze was poured into clay and sand moulds, where it hardened into solid bronze.

Molten bronze is liquid and can be poured into moulds to produce a variety of objects, such as knives and axe heads.

The rise of bronze

At first, bronze was extremely valuable because it was rare. Few people knew how to create bronze objects, so they were hard to come by. Also, it could only be produced in areas rich in metal. Only wealthy, powerful people could afford bronze objects, such as jewellery. As bronze became more widely available, thanks to metal trading routes (see page 21), new weapons, such as the sword, were developed. For the first time in history, warriors wore protective metal armour, including helmets and shields.

Rich Europeans from the Bronze Age showed off their wealth by wearing bronze jewellery, belt buckles and cloak brooches. They carried bronze swords and daggers.

9

IRON

People began to make iron in around 1200 BCE in the Middle East and southwestern Europe. By 700 BCE, ironworking had spread across Europe. Iron was more easily available than bronze, which made strong iron tools and weapons more accessible to many Iron Age people.

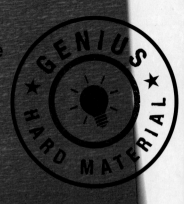

GENIUS ★ HARD MATERIAL ★

A different process

Iron ore is more common than copper and tin ores so Iron Age people didn't have to import the ore from other areas. However, extracting iron from its ore is more difficult than copper or tin. Iron Age people found that iron couldn't be melted and poured like bronze. Instead, pieces of iron ore had to be heated to a very high temperature with charcoal. Then, they were hammered into shape while red-hot.

WOW!

The first iron used to make tools was taken from meteorites that fell to Earth from space! These meteorites were pure iron, so the metal didn't need to be processed before it could be used. Meteorite iron was used in the Middle East, China and northern Canada.

This modern blacksmith is hammering iron while it is red-hot to give it its shape. This is the same technique that was used in the Iron Age.

Iron Age people used iron to make weapons, as well as for cooking pots and utensils.

From bronze to iron

During the Iron Age, bronze weapons and tools were replaced with iron ones fairly quickly. This may have been due to improved contact with other groups, which helped iron-making technology to spread fast. It may have also been due to a shortage of tin, which prevented people from making bronze. The strength and availability of iron made it the obvious choice for new weapons and tools.

Farming with iron

Iron tools and weapons were stronger and more effective than those made of bronze. Iron Age people used their new iron tools to cut down large numbers of trees to create more farmland. They then used iron farming tools to break up the heavy soil, so that they could grow crops. In this way, the development of iron tools helped them to produce more food and support a larger number of people.

Iron Age farmers used iron-tipped wooden ploughs to prepare the fields before planting seeds.

FARMING

In around 10,000 BCE, Stone Age people began to farm the land and grow crops, rather than just eating wild foods. This change had a huge impact on society, affecting the movement of people, population size and settlements.

GENIUS
★ ★ STABLE FOOD SUPPLY

Hunter-gatherers

The first humans were hunter-gatherers. They moved around looking for wild food, including animals to hunt, and leaves, fruits and roots to collect. The food they ate depended on their location and the season, for example berries in autumn. If food was hard to find, a group would move on to a new location.

Blackberries, birds' eggs and young nettles are some wild foods that Stone Age people in Europe would have eaten.

12

The first farmers

Around 10,000 BCE, people in Turkey, the Middle East and Mesopotamia began to farm. They planted fields of crops, such as barley and early types of wheat. They domesticated animals, such as sheep, goats and cattle, for their meat and milk. These farms allowed people to produce much more food than they could have collected in the wild. Over time, farming spread across Asia and Europe.

A changing world

The development of farming led to changes in society. Humans could grow enough food to support a larger population. As a result, the number of humans grew around the world. Groups had to settle in one place to look after their farms. They built permanent villages next to their fields with more complex houses and structures (see page 14).

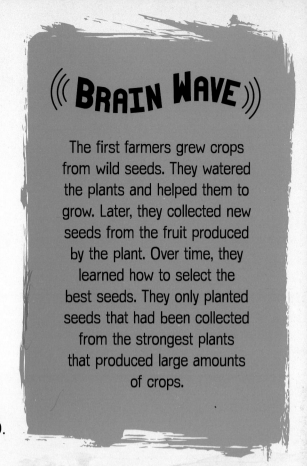

(((BRAIN WAVE)))

The first farmers grew crops from wild seeds. They watered the plants and helped them to grow. Later, they collected new seeds from the fruit produced by the plant. Over time, they learned how to select the best seeds. They only planted seeds that had been collected from the strongest plants that produced large amounts of crops.

This artist's impression shows a Bronze Age farming village in around 2000 BCE. There are livestock and a few fields of crops.

CONSTRUCTION

When humans settled down in one place to farm in the late Stone Age and Bronze Age, they built permanent structures nearby to live in. Farming freed up extra time for people to experiment with different building materials and other types of structure.

GENIUS
★ PERMANENT BUILDINGS ★

Simple shelters

As hunter-gatherers did not stay in one place for long, they built quick, temporary shelters. They set up camp in the mouths of caves or built simple structures from leaves, sticks and animal skins. Later in the Stone Age, some groups would return to the same place every year. They started to build more complex camps that they could come back to.

Construction techniques

When farmers started to build permanent settlements, they put more time and energy into constructing better shelters, as they knew they would be there for some time. These shelters looked different around the world, depending on the materials available such as wood, stone or mud. People developed different building techniques using these materials. Some made bricks from dried mud or packed dried straw closely together to make a thatched roof.

In the Bronze Age, people in the UK built permanent houses from wood and thatch.

14

Monuments and megaliths

As well as houses, people began to construct other types of building. Many groups of people around the world built huge monuments, frequently for religious reasons. These monuments were often made of giant stones, called megaliths. In the Bronze Age, the Sumerians built huge buildings called ziggurats in Mesopotamia. The bricks in the ziggurats were arranged in steps that got gradually smaller towards the top (see page 5).

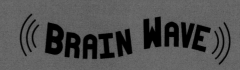

BRAIN WAVE

Historians aren't sure how the makers of Stonehenge lifted the very heavy stones. They may have built wooden scaffolding to lift them up bit by bit or pushed them up on ramps. However they did it, it was a brilliant piece of engineering work!

Stonehenge in England has a ring of standing megaliths, some with stones balanced on top.

SETTLEMENTS

Over time, the first Stone Age farming settlements grew into small villages. These villages became centres of industry, with workshops for craftsmen. In the Bronze and Iron Ages, some of these villages grew into towns and even cities, where thousands of people lived close together.

WOW!

The site of the current city of Jericho, Palestine has been inhabited for 10,000 years. This makes it one of the oldest continuously inhabited towns in the world!

New roles

With the development of farming, a smaller number of people could produce enough food to feed a large population. This freed up people to work on other projects. Some became potters, craftspeople and metal workers, producing pots, fabric and weapons. Others became warriors to defend their village against attacks from other tribes. A few became priests, who led religious rituals and celebrations.

People in a Stone Age farming village had different roles. Some were farmers, while others made tools, caught fish or prepared food.

This hill fort was built in the southwest of England during the Iron Age. Families lived in houses at the top of the central mound.

Keeping safe

Towns and cities offered protection to Bronze and Iron Age people. There was safety in numbers, as warriors and men from the town would defend it in the event of an attack. Defensive walls were built around some settlements to keep residents safe.

(((BRAIN WAVE)))

High settlements are easier to defend, as you can see your enemies coming and have the advantage of fighting battles downhill. In Bronze and Iron Age Europe, some groups built hill forts on tall hills. They dug ditches around their settlements to make it even harder for attackers to reach them at the top.

Special towns

Over time, some Bronze and Iron Age towns and cities developed specialities. Settlements near resources, such as metal, became manufacturing centres, home to craftspeople trained to work with these resources. Settlements near rivers or on the coast became trading centres (see page 21). Traders brought in new and unusual goods from far away, and exchanged them for locally produced objects.

SOCIETY

During the Stone, Bronze and Iron Ages, society changed from being relatively equal to hierarchical, with rulers at the top and others in order of importance underneath. While leaders enjoyed a more comfortable lifestyle, ordinary people did not share the same luxuries as those at the top.

GENIUS
ORGANISED SOCIETY

An equal society?

Historians can only guess about the society of the first Stone Age humans. As hunter-gatherers, everyone in society had the same responsibility — collecting and preparing food to eat. For this reason, most people probably saw each other as equals. Archaeologists have found evidence that even in the late Stone Age, people lived in houses of the same size. This is a sign of a relatively equal society.

Skara Brae is a Stone Age village on the Scottish island of Orkney. The houses that remain are all exactly the same size and have the same features.

The beginnings of wealth

As farming became widespread, the people who controlled the extra food produced by farming became powerful and wealthy. When bronze was introduced, these powerful people were the first to obtain metal objects. This was the beginning of a hierarchical society. The people at the top of society had valuable items and more food, while ordinary people lived much simpler and more basic lives.

This is a recreation of a Bronze Age grave found in Varna, Bulgaria. The person was buried with many gold items, probably because of their high status.

Iron Age hierarchy

By the beginning of the Iron Age, there were many different roles in society, each with its own level of importance. Tribal leaders were at the top, followed by noble people and priests underneath. Below them were warriors and skilled craftspeople. Landless labourers and slaves were at the bottom. People from each part of society lived in houses of different sizes, wore different clothes and ate different foods.

tribal leaders/kings

noble people

priests

warriors

skilled craftspeople

farmers/fishermen

landless labourers and slaves

TRADE

In the late Stone Age and early Bronze Age, people began to trade with each other to share resources. Groups traded surplus food supplies, craft products and specific resources, such as tin, that could only be found in certain areas.

Stone Age sharing

After the introduction of farming, Stone Age people had surplus food for the first time. Some food was dried and stored for later use, while some was traded with other groups in the local area. People also traded resources, such as flint, and craft products, which could be made in excess due to the extra time freed up by farming.

WOW!

Archaeologists have found Stone Age jade axes in Scotland that originally came from the Italian Alps!

Valuable stones, such as obsidian from the Greek islands, and amber from Poland, were traded across Stone Age Europe.

obsidian   amber

Trading tin

In the Bronze Age, trading became very important because tin, one of the raw materials needed for bronze, was only found in a few areas, such as Cornwall, Tuscany and eastern Portugal. Bronze Age people across Europe depended on trade with these areas to be able to make the bronze needed for tools and weapons. Bronze Age traders across Europe and Asia became rich from trading tin, as well as precious metals and textiles.

This necklace found in a Sumerian royal tomb is made from traded, non-local materials. It has beads made from lapis lazuli, from what is now Afghanistan, and gold from what is now Iran and Turkey.

Land and sea

By the Iron Age, a network of trade routes had been established across Europe, allowing goods to be transported by land or sea. This gave people access to a wider variety of foods and objects. Commonly traded goods included salt and amber, a gemstone used for jewellery. Iron Age tribes traded goods with each other, as well as with large civilisations, such as the ancient Greeks.

Iron Age traders in the Mediterranean probably used simple wooden ships, similar to this modern replica.

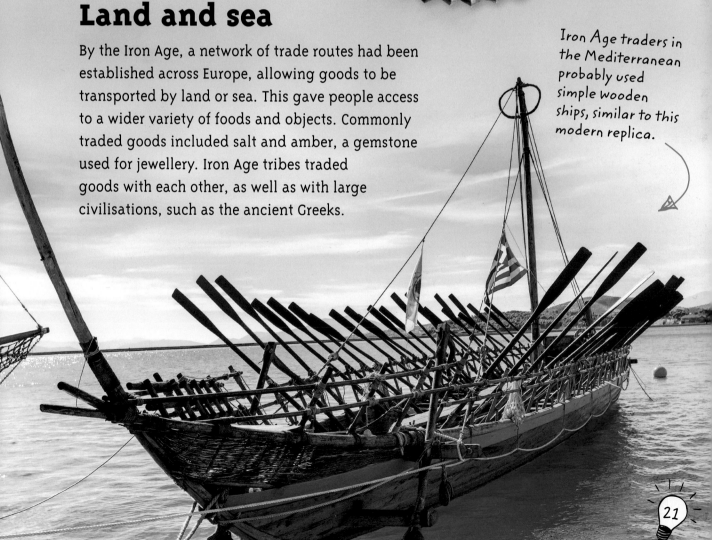

CLOTHING

We don't have much information about the clothing worn during the Stone, Bronze and Iron Ages. Most ancient textiles have rotted away and are very rarely found. However, by looking at the technologies used to make clothes, we can guess what people wore.

GENIUS ★ NATURAL GARMENTS

Knives and needles

The first humans kept warm by covering themselves in animal skins. They used stone knives to cut the skin from the animals. The development of needles, made from bone or horn, enabled people to make holes in these skins. They could now make fitted clothes from animal skins sewn together with thin pieces of leather or plants. These clothes kept people warmer, which allowed them to travel into colder climates.

This artist's impression shows Stone Age people in different clothes made from animal skins, including boots to protect their feet.

Weaving

Over time, people started making their own material. They wove baskets and fishing nets from plant fibre. By 5000 BCE, people were weaving cloth fabric from threads made from plant and animal fibres. The threads used to make cloth varied across the world. In India, they used cotton, while in China, they used silk. People in other areas, such as Britain, wove cloth from wool. They used natural dyes from plants to colour the cloth.

(((BRAIN WAVE)))

At first, people made thread by hand. They rolled animal hair or plants in their hands until it became thin threads. Thread making became easier later in the Stone Age, thanks to the drop spindle. A drop spindle is a weighted stick, through which fibres are threaded.

The loom

Stone Age people used looms to weave fabric. A loom was a wooden frame that was set up with strings of thread hanging vertically from the top. Stones were tied to the bottom of each string to keep it straight. Threads were woven horizontally back and forth between the vertical threads to create large pieces of woven fabric. These large pieces of fabric could be made into different types of clothes.

The weight of the spindle pulls the fibre into thin thread when it is spun. The thread is then wrapped around the spindle.

This is a replica of an ancient loom. A weaver could walk around the loom while weaving to reach either side.

TEST of TIME

Woven fabric is still created in exactly the same way, with horizontal threads wrapped around vertical threads. However, since the Industrial Revolution in the eighteenth century, people have used mechanical looms that create fabric automatically. Some craftspeople still weave by hand, producing high-quality luxury fabrics.

ART

Some historians believe that the moment at which our Stone Age ancestors became human was when they started to create art. This is because animals do not create art – only humans do. Art became more and more sophisticated throughout the Bronze Age and Iron Age. People created elaborately decorated objects as symbols of wealth and power.

The first paintings

Cave painting was one of the earliest forms of art in the Stone Age. People painted pictures of animals, and occasionally humans, on walls deep inside caves. They used red, brown and black paints, made from charcoal and soil. These paintings may have had a religious or symbolic meaning.

This cave painting of a bison in Altamira, Spain, was painted over 15,000 years ago. Bison lived across Europe in the Stone Age but they are now extinct in this area.

New materials

Every new material that humans learned how to work with was used to create art and decorative objects. In the Stone Age, people carved bone into figurines and beads for jewellery. After the development of pottery, people made decorative sculptures, as well as functional pots. In the Bronze and Iron Ages, craftspeople made brooches and rings from metal.

This Sumerian headdress is made from gold and precious stones and dates back to around 2600–2500 BCE.

Decorating the world

In the Bronze and Iron Ages, artistic decoration was also added to functional objects, such as weapons, chariots and bowls. This decoration would have taken extra time and resources, making the decorated object more expensive. These objects would have been symbols of power, only owned by wealthy, important people at the top of society.

TEST OF TIME

Men and women around the world still wear jewellery made from the same materials that people used thousands of years ago, such as metal and precious stones. Today, people also make jewellery from man-made materials, such as plastic.

This sword from roughly 60 BCE, is decorated with a warrior on the handle.

25

THE WHEEL

The invention of the wheel actually happened relatively late. Humans were building complex boats and doing complicated metalwork before the wheel was invented.

GENIUS ★ NEW WAY TO MOVE ★

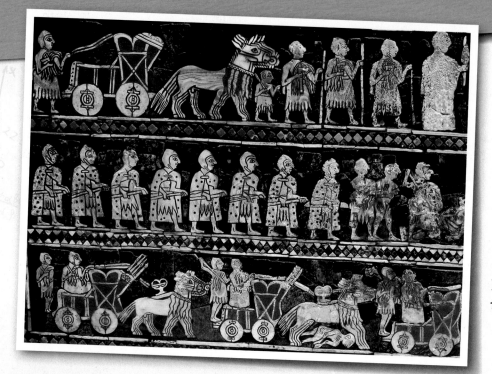

This decorated Sumerian box, known as the Standard of Ur, shows soldiers and wheeled wagons on their way to battle. It dates back to 2600 BCE.

The first wheels

Some historians believe that the first wheels were potter's wheels built in around 3500 BCE in Mesopotamia. The potter smoothed each pot as it spun on the wheel, to make it a more regular shape. These wheels were solid discs with a hole in the centre for the axle. The axle and the hole in the wheel had to be perfectly smooth, or the friction between the parts would stop the wheel from spinning correctly.

Moving around

The first wheeled vehicles appeared in Mesopotamia in around 3000 BCE. They were possibly inspired by potter's wheels, or by log rollers used to move heavy objects. Wheeled vehicles made it much easier to transport heavy goods over long distances. Carts were pulled by oxen or donkeys, as there were no domesticated horses in Mesopotamia at the time. The wheels on these carts were solid wood, which made the vehicle quite heavy.

Riding into battle

Two developments — the invention of the spoked wheel, with rods that connect to the centre to the rim, and the domestication of the horse — were key to the invention of the horse-drawn chariot in around 2000 BCE. Spoked wheels were much lighter than solid wheels, which made the chariots easier to pull at faster speeds. Horses could also travel quicker than oxen, pulling the chariot at top speed. This made the chariot a valuable weapon in battle.

TEST of TIME

Eventually, cavalry soldiers mounted on horseback became more widespread than soldiers in chariots. However, chariots were still used for transport and for entertainment, such as the chariot races that were popular in ancient Greece and Rome.

When the Roman Emperor, Julius Caesar, tried to invade Britain in 54 BCE, the Britons drove chariots in battle against him. They used the chariots to break up the ranks of Roman soldiers and then jumped off and fought hand-to-hand.

WRITING

The earliest human communication was spoken language, probably used by the first modern humans who lived in tropical Africa 180,000 years ago. Humans communicated in this way for thousands of years before writing began. Writing was a huge step forward for communication. People began to keep written records, which tell us about the lives of ancient people.

GENIUS ★ COMMUNICATION RECORDS ★

Sumerian symbols

In ancient Mesopotamia in around 3500 BCE, people used small clay models to keep track of farming and trade records. These models were kept in clay envelopes. Eventually, people began to draw the contents of the envelope on the outside, which meant that the models weren't needed any more. The drawing was enough to represent the information that the writer wanted to communicate. These symbols, or pictographs, were the first form of writing.

Sounding it out

However, there were some words and ideas that could not be drawn in a picture, such as names. So, the Sumerians started to use symbols for words that sounded the same to sound out words that couldn't be drawn. For example, the Sumerian word for hand was 'su', so they drew a hand when they wanted to refer to a hand or to represent 'su' when the sound appeared in other words.

The first writing was used for farming records, such as the amount of wheat harvested from a field.

vase

This Sumerian tablet records the transfer of land. It's thought the vase and foot symbols were used to represent sounds, while the image of plants represented a garden.

plants

foot

28

Developing an alphabet

One of the first complete writing systems was ancient Egyptian hieroglyphics, which combined pictographs, representing objects, and characters that represented sounds, like an alphabet. This allowed people to keep detailed, accurate records of things that could not be drawn. Eventually, around 1500 BCE, scribes developed an alphabet in which each letter represented a sound. This system was more convenient as fewer symbols were needed.

TEST OF TIME

The Romans brought their language, Latin, and their alphabet with them as they conquered land across Europe. Today, the Latin alphabet is used by about 70 per cent of people to write their own language.

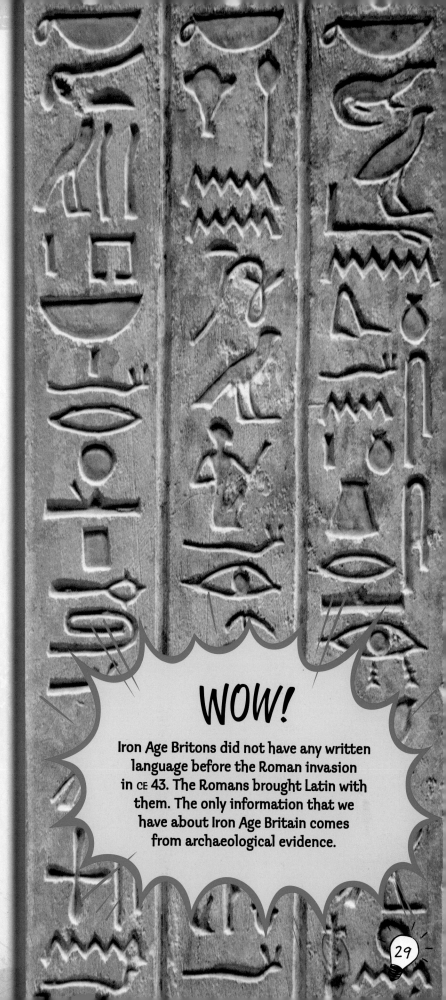

WOW!

Iron Age Britons did not have any written language before the Roman invasion in CE 43. The Romans brought Latin with them. The only information that we have about Iron Age Britain comes from archaeological evidence.

Some Egyptian hieroglyphics represented objects and sounds. For example, the wavy line represented water and the 'n' sound.

GLOSSARY

alloy — a mixture of different elements, including at least one metal

ancestor — a relative who lived a long time ago

axle — the pole in the centre of a circular object that allows it to spin around

DNA — genetic information

domesticate — to control previously wild animals or plants and use them for food or work

flint — a type of shiny stone

hierarchy — a system in which things are organised according to their importance

hill fort — a settlement built on top of a hill with walls or ditches to defend it from attack

hunter-gatherer — someone who moves around to find wild food to eat and doesn't settle in one place

loom — a machine used to weave thread into fabric

megalith — a large stone

Mesopotamia — an area mainly in what is now known as Iraq

molten — melted

ore — rock or soil from which metal can be extracted

pictograph — a picture used to represent something

prehistoric — describing the time before written records

raw material — a natural material that has not yet been made into something else

serrated — describes a blade with several sharp points along its edge

Sumerians — a civilisation that lived in Mesopotamia in the Bronze Age

thatch — a building material made of straw or dried plants

TIMELINE

STONE AGE

3.3 million years ago	Stones are first used as tools.
1.8 million years ago	Early humans start to move out of Africa.
9000 BCE	The end of the last Ice Age brings warmer temperatures.
10,000 BCE	Farming begins in the Middle East.

BRONZE AGE

4000 BCE	The first bronze is produced in what is now Turkey.
3100 BCE	The earliest types of writing appear in ancient Mesopotamia (modern day southern Iraq) and ancient Egypt.
3000 BCE	The first potter's wheels and wheeled vehicles are used in Mesopotamia.
2000 BCE	The use of bronze becomes widespread across the Middle East and Europe.
2000 BCE	The horse-drawn chariot is invented.

IRON AGE

1200 BCE	People begin to work with iron in the Middle East and southwestern Europe.
700 BCE	Ironworking has spread across Europe.

INDEX

FURTHER INFORMATION

Websites

www.dkfindout.com/uk/history/stone-age/

www.bbc.co.uk/guides/z874kqt

www.theschoolrun.com/homework-help/the-iron-age

Books

Explore! Stone, Bronze and Iron Ages by Sonya Newland (Wayland, 2017)

Prehistoric Adventures series by John Malam (Wayland, 2017)

Found! Stone Age, Bronze Age and Iron Age by Moira Butterfield (Franklin Watts, 2017)